10 WEDDING DUETS

- Air on the G String…………………J. S. Bach
- Bridal Chorus…………………………Wagner
- Canon in D……………………………Pachelbel
- Clair de Lune……………………………Debussy
- The Four Seasons (Spring)…………..Vivaldi
- Jesu, Joy of Man's Desiring…….J. S. Bach
- Ode to Joy……………………………Beethoven
- Prelude no. 1 in C……………….....J. S. Bach
- Trumpet Voluntary………………..Clarke
- Wedding March……………..Mendelsohn

Arranged by B. C. Dockery

© 2021

Air on the G String

J. S. Bach
arr. B. C. Dockery

Violin I

Air on the G String

J. S. Bach
arr. B. C. Dockery

Air on the G String

Violin II

J. S. Bach
arr. B. C. Dockery

Air on the G String

Piano

J. S. Bach
arr. B. C. Dockery

Air on the G String

Bridal Chorus

Richard Wagner
arr. B. C. Dockery

Bridal Chorus

Violin I

Bridal Chorus

Richard Wagner
arr. B. C. Dockery

Bridal Chorus

Violin II

Richard Wagner
arr. B. C. Dockery

Bridal Chorus

Piano

Richard Wagner
arr. B. C. Dockery

Bridal Chorus

rit.

Canon in D

Johann Pachelbel
arr. B. C. Dockery

Canon in D

Canon in D

Violin I

Canon in D

Johann Pachelbel
arr. B. C. Dockery

Canon in D

Violin II

Canon in D

Johann Pachelbel
arr. B. C. Dockery

2

Canon in D

Piano

Canon in D

Johann Pachelbel
arr. B. C. Dockery

Canon in D

Canon in D

Clair de Lune

Claude Debussy
arr. B. C. Dockery

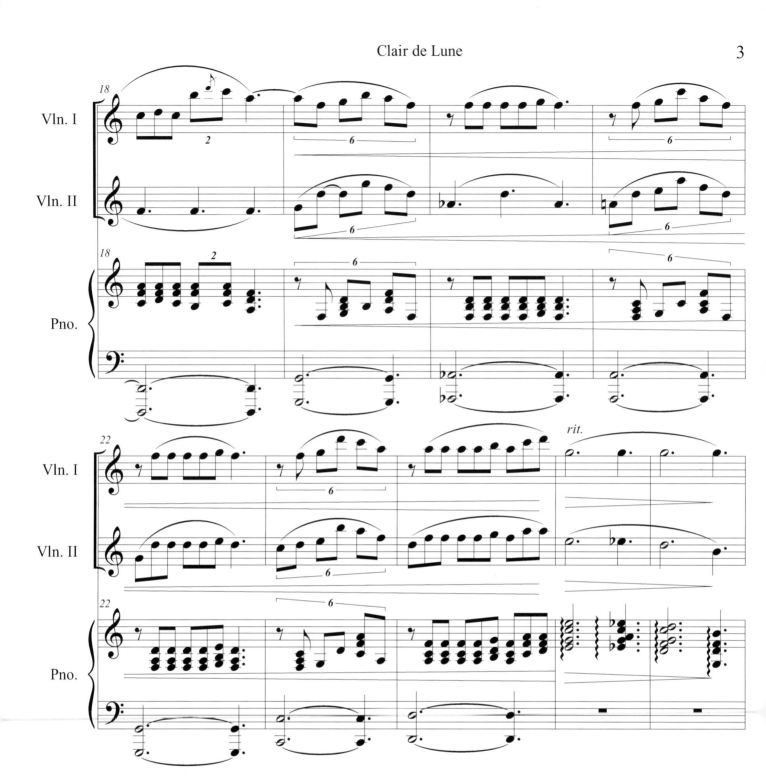

4

Clair de Lune

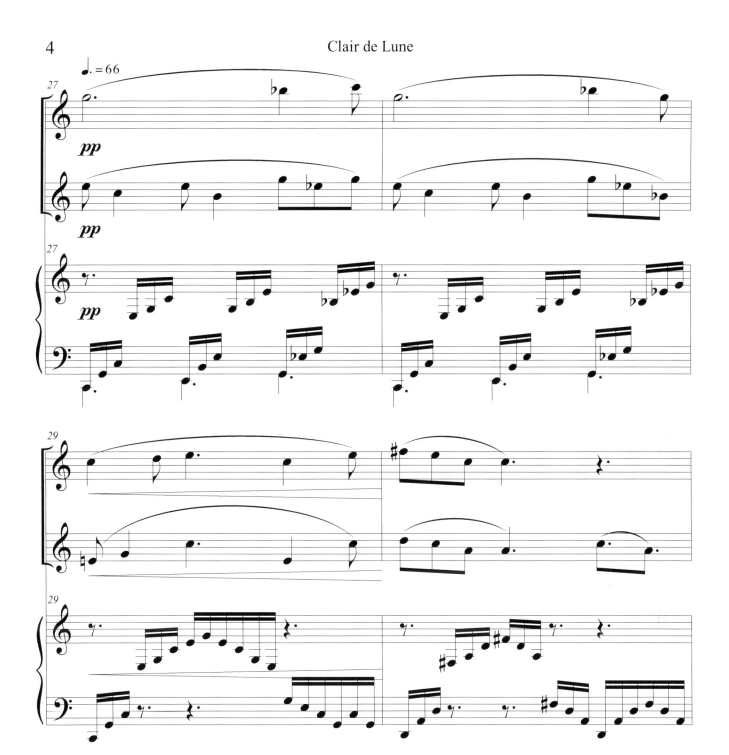

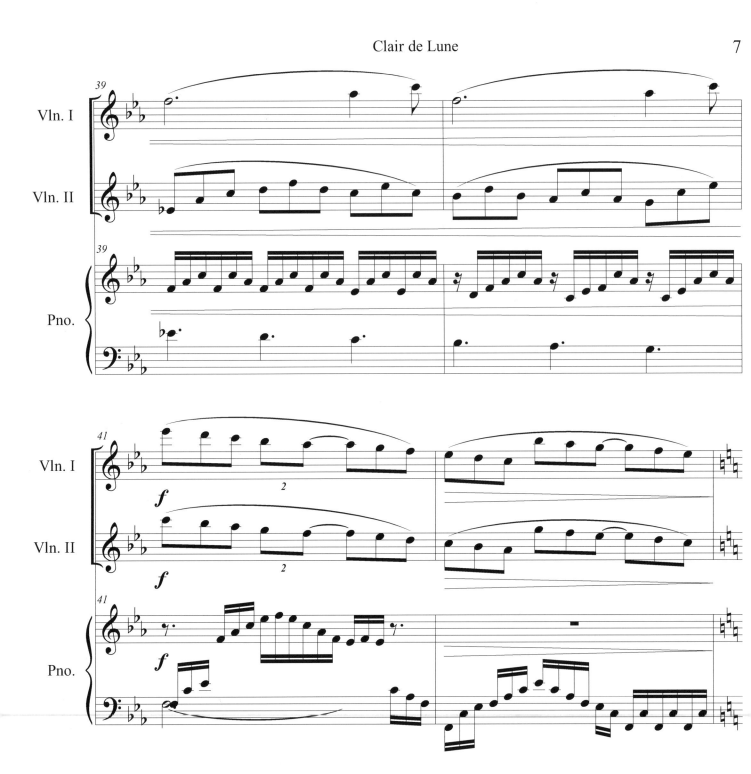

Clair de Lune

Clair de Lune

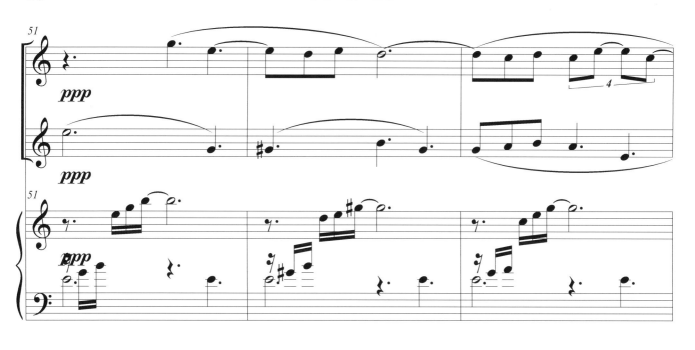

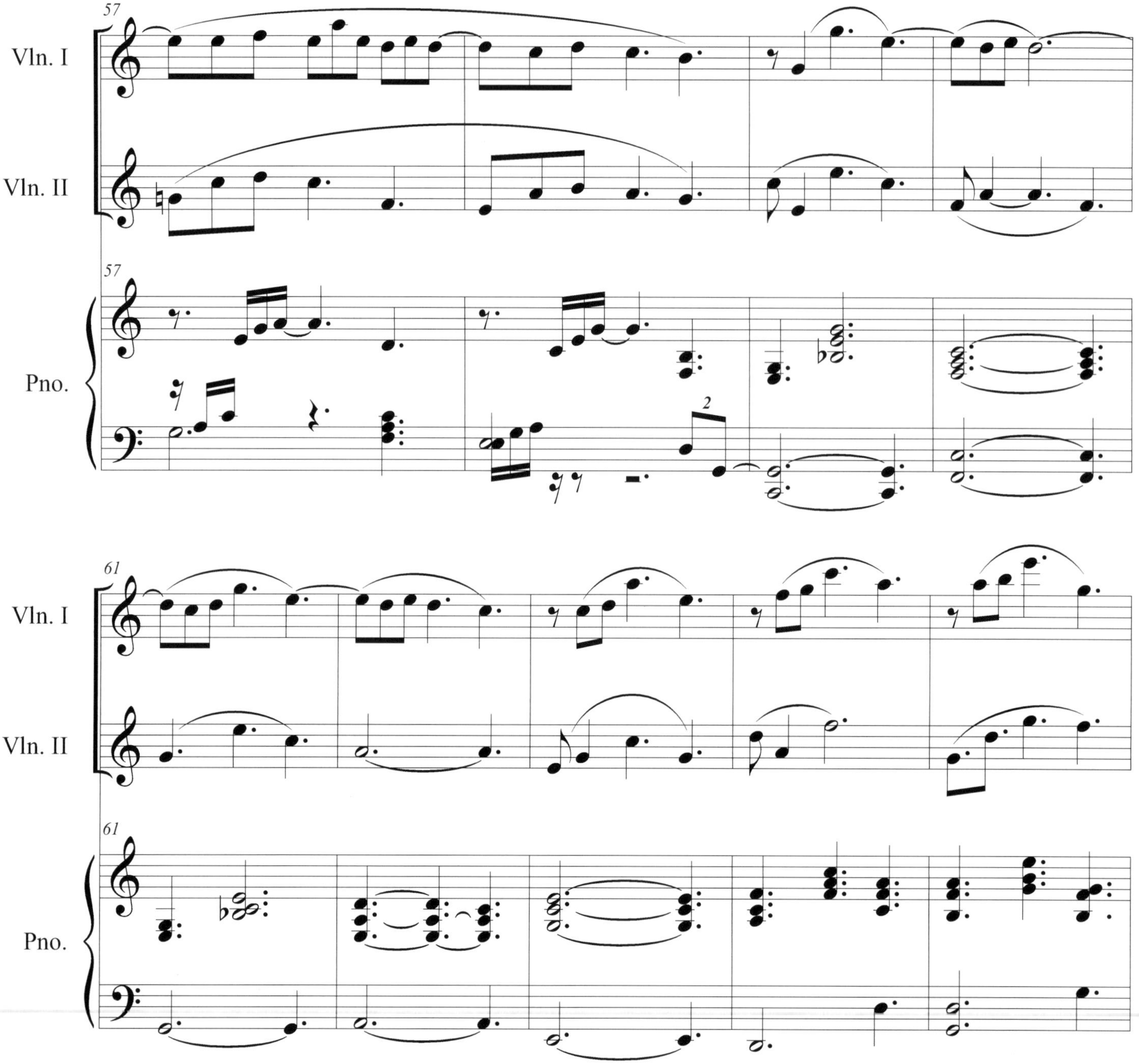
57
Vln. I
Vln. II
57
Pno.
2
61
Vln. I
Vln. II
61
Pno.

Clair de Lune

Violin I

Clair de Lune

Claude Debussy
arr. B. C. Dockery

Clair de Lune

Violin II

Clair de Lune

Claude Debussy
arr. B. C. Dockery

Clair de Lune

Clair de Lune

Piano

Claude Debussy
arr. B. C. Dockery

©2021

Clair de Lune

Clair de Lune

Spring from the Four Seasons

Antonio Vivaldi
arr. B. C. Dockery

©2021

Allegro (M.M. ♩= c. 140)

Spring from the Four Seasons

Violin I

Antonio Vivaldi
arr. B. C. Dockery

Spring from the Four Seasons

Violin II

Antonio Vivaldi
arr. B. C. Dockery

Allegro (M.M. ♩ = c. 140)

Spring from the Four Seasons

Piano

Antonio Vivaldi
arr. B. C. Dockery

Allegro (M.M. ♩ = c. 140)

Jesu, Joy of Man's Desiring

J. S. Bach
arr. B. C. Dockery

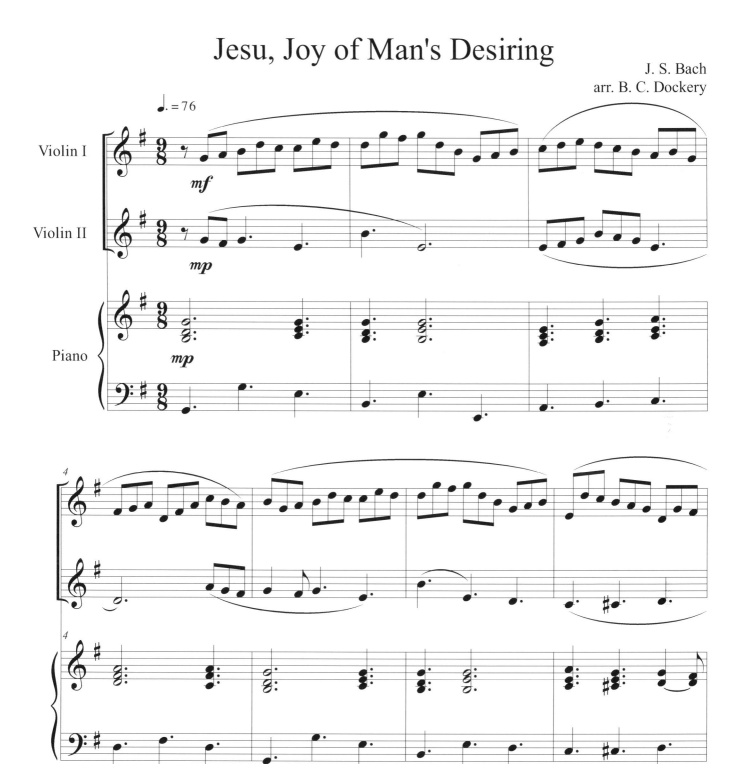

Jesu, Joy of Man's Desiring

Jesu, Joy of Man's Desiring

Violin I

J. S. Bach
arr. B. C. Dockery

Jesu, Joy of Man's Desiring

Violin II

J. S. Bach
arr. B. C. Dockery

Jesu, Joy of Man's Desiring

Piano

J. S. Bach
arr. B. C. Dockery

Jesu, Joy of Man's Desiring

Ode to Joy
(Joyful, Joyful, We Adore Thee)

Beethoven
arr. B. C. Dockery

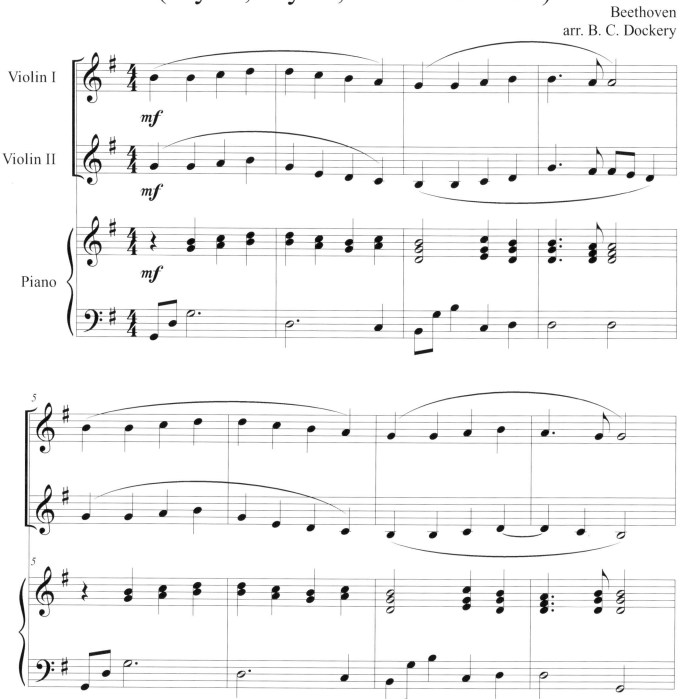

Ode to Joy
(Joyful, Joyful, We Adore Thee)

Ode to Joy
(Joyful, Joyful, We Adore Thee)

Violin I

Beethoven
arr. B. C. Dockery

Ode to Joy
(Joyful, Joyful, We Adore Thee)

Violin II

Beethoven
arr. B. C. Dockery

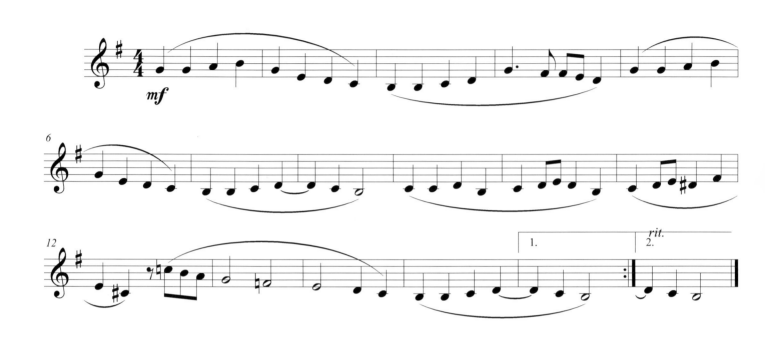

©2021

Ode to Joy
(Joyful, Joyful, We Adore Thee)

Piano

Beethoven
arr. B. C. Dockery

Prelude No. 1
from the Well-Tempered Clavier Bk 1

J. S. Bach
arr. B. C. Dockery

Prelude No. 1
from the Well-Tempered Clavier Bk 1

Prelude No. 1
from the Well-Tempered Clavier Bk 1

Prelude No. 1
from the Well-Tempered Clavier Bk 1

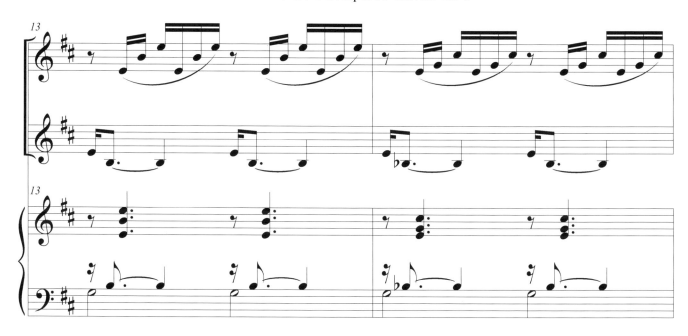

Prelude No. 1
from the Well-Tempered Clavier Bk 1

Prelude No. 1
from the Well-Tempered Clavier Bk 1

Prelude No. 1
from the Well-Tempered Clavier Bk 1

Prelude No. 1
from the Well-Tempered Clavier Bk 1

Prelude No. 1
from the Well-Tempered Clavier Bk 1

Prelude No. 1
from the Well-Tempered Clavier Bk 1

Violin I

J. S. Bach
arr. B. C. Dockery

Prelude No. 1
from the Well-Tempered Clavier Bk 1

Prelude No. 1
from the Well-Tempered Clavier Bk 1

Violin II

J. S. Bach
arr. B. C. Dockery

Prelude No. 1
from the Well-Tempered Clavier Bk 1

Prelude No. 1
from the Well-Tempered Clavier Bk 1

Piano

J. S. Bach
arr. B. C. Dockery

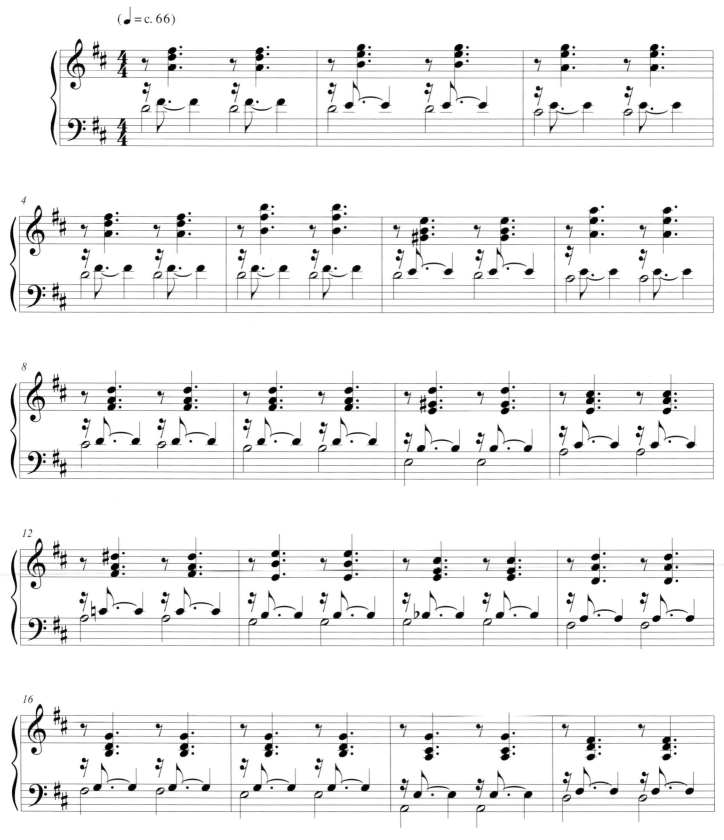

2

Prelude No. 1
from the Well-Tempered Clavier Bk 1

rit.

Trumpet Voluntary

Jeremy Clark
arr. B. C. Dockery

Trumpet Voluntary

Trumpet Voluntary

Violin I

Jeremy Clark
arr. B. C. Dockery

Trumpet Voluntary

Violin II

Jeremy Clark
arr. B. C. Dockery

Trumpet Voluntary

Piano

Jeremy Clark
arr. B. C. Dockery

Trumpet Voluntary

Wedding March

Felix Mendelssohn
arr. B. C. Dockery

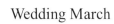

Wedding March

Violin I

Felix Mendelssohn
arr. B. C. Dockery

Violin II

Wedding March

Felix Mendelssohn
arr. B. C. Dockery

Wedding March

Piano

Felix Mendelssohn
arr. B. C. Dockery

Wedding March

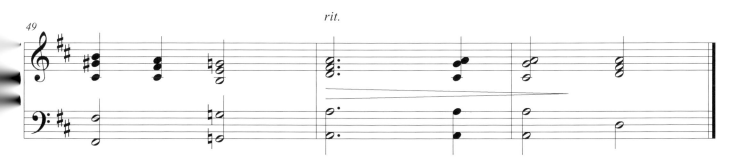

Made in the USA
Columbia, SC
13 September 2022

67152931R00067